Kids Shenanigans

Great Things to Do That Mom and Dad Will Just Barely Approve Of

by the editors of Klutz Press

illustrated by H. B. Lewis
and Sara Boore

Klutz Press   Palo Alto, California

Cartoon illustrations © 1992 by
H.B. Lewis

Instructional art by Sara Boore

Book design by
MaryEllen Podgorski

Book manufactured in South Korea.
Whoopee cushion kit made in
Taiwan.

ISBN 1-878257-41-2

Grateful acknowledgements to
Martin Gardner, Jeff Busby, Scott
Morris, Patrick Ryan, Paul Doherty
and Bernd Kutzscher.

Write Us. Klutz Press is an
independent publisher located in
Palo Alto, California and staffed
entirely by real human beings.
We would love to hear your
comments regarding this, or
any of our other books.

Klutz Press
2121 Staunton Court
Palo Alto, CA 94306

4 1 5 8 5 7 0 8 8

List of Shenanigans

Introduction   4

Hanging Spoons   5

The One Finger Grown-up Hoist   6

The Best Paper Airplane
You Can Make   8

The Grape-Through-Your-Head
Trick   13

Hand Jive   14

Upside-Down Water   19

Homemade Whoopee
Cushion   20

Fake a Sneeze   21

How to Flip a Coin
with Triumphant Style   22

Tennis Ball Launcher   25

Flinch and Stink Eye   26

Snapping Belt Loops   28

Dead Finger   29

Paper Poppers   30

Hand Whistling   32

The Parent and the Egg   35

How to Sneak Around   36

The Egg and Shirt Throw   41

Phone Code   42

Pig Latin   44

Oppish   45

Grown-up Stumpers   46

Be Your Own Soda Can
Bomb Squad   49

Fun in the Mail   50

Kid Facts   52

Body Weirdnesses and Tongue
Gymnastics   54

Dollar Ring   56

The Coat Hanger and the Coin   61

The Automatic (Systematic)
Articulated Mop and Spring-
Loaded Broom-Driven Pie Tin Flyer
and Egg Dropper   64

Introduction

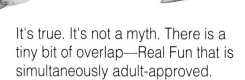

There are two kinds of fun in this world—Adult-Approved Grown-up Fun ... and Real Fun.

They are quite different.

We came to this shocking realization after nearly three years of grueling shenanigan research. On the adult side, we interviewed many leading grown-ups, with typical leading grown-up attitudes. On the kid side, we sought out some of the country's premier class clowns—detention room veterans with scary, district-wide reputations.

Looking back over all this, we can summarize our findings as follows: What kids and teens *really* want to do, and what their parents are prepared to let them do, are almost entirely not the same things. This, of course, is common knowledge to both groups, but it was interesting to see it so scientifically verified.

But notice we said "*almost* entirely not the same things."

It's true. It's not a myth. There is a tiny bit of overlap—Real Fun that is simultaneously adult-approved.

What we resolved to do was ex-plore this small bit of overlap more fully than any before us We searched for those rare activities deep in the heart of the Real Fun Zone, yet still on this side of the Parent Approval Line.

Or at least close to it.

Now that the collection is ready to go to press, we find ourselves enormously proud of this proudly immature collection. It is like no other in print. If it were a kid though, heaven help us all.

Hanging Spoons

According to archaeologists who have studied the matter, this shenanigan has roots that go back to the ancient Egyptians, who would hang spoons from their noses in the course of performing specific rites in honor of Shoo-Ha-Ra, their god of china and flatware.

It is best performed at the dinner table.

During a lull in the conversation, share with everyone the historical fact stated above and ask if anyone there is capable of performing this ancient feat. Chances are good, a few people will try. Chances are also good, they will fail miserably. But keep encouraging them. There is almost nothing better for perking up a dull meal than watching everyone try to hang spoons from their noses.

When your fellow diners are thus engaged, discreetly lick the tip of your finger and rub it on the end of your nose. Don't worry, this is not disgusting. Then breathe once or twice on the bowl of your spoon, so it fogs up the silver. Wait a moment for everything to dry.

Announce that you have seen enough silliness and you will now demonstrate the proper technique. Wave the spoon around for effect. Breathe deeply. Cross your eyes. Say something in Egyptian. Lean your head back a bit and press the spoon firmly onto your nose where your dried slobber will enable it to stick just enough.

Bring your head slowly down. Bask in the applause.

The One Finger Grown-up Hoist

This extremely baffling shenanigan was first described in 1655 in a diary kept by the Englishman Samuel Pepys. From time to time over the years, other written accounts of it have been published, often in books devoted to flying saucers, Loch Ness monsters, and other fun phenomena.

Here is how it goes: A big kid (or smallish grown-up) is asked to stand on two books.

Be sure there's some space beneath foot.

Let's make Mom the subject grown-up. Four kids assemble around her. Two of them squat down behind her; the other two stand at her sides. The kids at her sides put a finger under her elbows (her arms are bent, and she is holding them stiffly). The two kids at her feet each put their forefingers under her feet between the two books. Then they attempt to raise Mom off the ground. Not too surprisingly, not too much happens.

Then it's time for a little hocus-pocus. The kids go off in a huddle.

They close their eyes. They chant secret chants. They breathe in and out deeply, together. Finally, they go back to Mom, put all of their hands over her eyes and ask her to lose a lot of weight instantly.

Then the kids get back to their stations. They take three deep breaths in unison. They ask Mom to close her eyes, hold her arms stiffly, and exhale every bit of breath. The fingers are put back in place and, *at the instant the third breath is taken*, all lift together.

Mom comes off the ground.

How come? Actually, there is still some argument over the explanation for this little amazement, despite the fact that it is 300 years old. Most observers think the biggest reason is the coordination of the second effort. With four kids, a 120 pound grown-up is only 30 pounds each *so long as the lifting is done simultaneously*. As for the "forefinger only" rule, that's really not much of a handicap at all, since an average human can lift virtually as much with his or her forefinger as with his full hand. On top of which, the ritual probably gets everyone to try a little harder. Add it all up, and UFOs probably account for only 10% of it.

P.S. If you have a fifth kid, get her or him to stand up on a chair and lift with a single finger right underneath the chin. Makes a nice touch and actually helps a good bit since heads are 20 pounds of dead weight.

The Best Paper Airplane You Can Make

Every school year, in the farthest back row in classrooms across our land, thousands of paper airplane designs are tested and launched, tested and launched, over and over again. This research is on-going every day.

Under these circumstances, to claim to have the very best design of all is obviously a big claim. But we think we can back it up.

Over the past 30 years, two major paper airplane contests have been held in this country. These two contests drew thousands of entries from all over the world, including a large number from aeronautical engineers, who presumably knew what they were doing. Both contests published their winners, which we have taken the liberty to categorize:

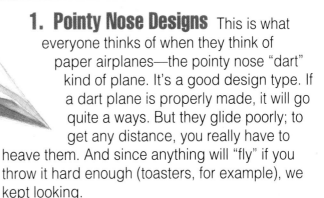

1. Pointy Nose Designs

This is what everyone thinks of when they think of paper airplanes—the pointy nose "dart" kind of plane. It's a good design type. If a dart plane is properly made, it will go quite a ways. But they glide poorly; to get any distance, you really have to heave them. And since anything will "fly" if you throw it hard enough (toasters, for example), we kept looking.

2. Oddball Designs

This second category contains all the miscellaneously strange designs, like flying rings, helicopters, etc. Interesting, but usually difficult to make and subject to frequent failure. Plus, they lack "airplane appearance." As a result, we passed on these designs as well.

3. Blunt Nose Gliders

Finally, the winning category. These are the very best, classroom quality, practical designs. These designs are tossed, not heaved like the darts. Plus, they float and fly in circles and long arcs. Much more interesting and much more "airplanelike."

After settling on the best category, we sifted through all the winning "blunt nose" gliders to find the one that performed the best for us. After much balcony research, we found the winner. It is folded out of plain paper. It doesn't need tape or paper clips. Its folds are simple and it flies like a dream. All in all, it is, by our own admission, The Best Paper Airplane You Can Make. Herewith, then, are our instructions:

Instructions for
The Best Paper Airplane You Can Make

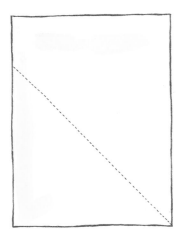

1. Fold up bottom left corner on dotted line.

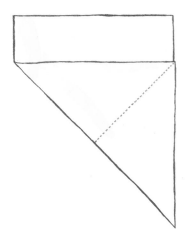

2. Fold up bottom right corner on dotted line...

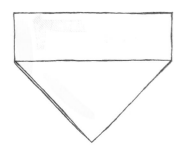

3. ...like this.

4. Flatten back out to a full sheet.

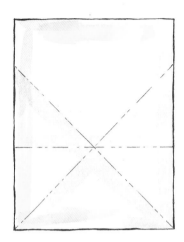

5. Fold and unfold on the horizontal line, leaving a crease. End up with a full sheet creased as shown.

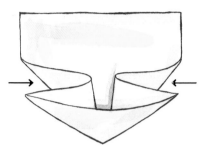

6. Fold up bottom, pushing in sides.

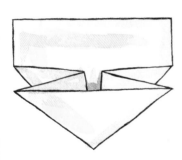

7. It will look like this.

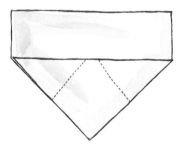

8. Press down firmly.

MORE!

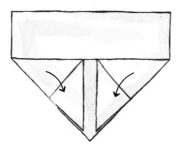

9. Fold down front flaps.

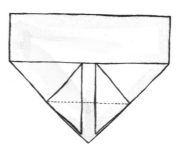

10. Fold up point on dotted line.

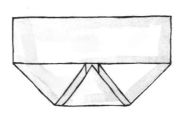

11. It will look like this.

fold at arrows

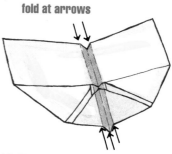

12. Make the body of your plane by folding a trough in the middle.

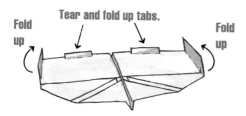

Fold up · Tear and fold up tabs. · Fold up

13. Now fold up the wing tips and tear and fold up tabs at the back.

To fly: Launch with a firm, straight-ahead throw. Naturally, if you can gain some elevation (if nothing else, stand up on your chair), you will experience far more success. If your plane circles hard, fool with the tabs on the wings until it flies the way you want.

The Grape-Through-Your-Head Trick

Reader! Do not skip this shenanigan; it's an instant path to immaturity. It is too dumb for words, but therein lies its greatness. Bonus! Absolutely no talent of any kind required.

Here is how it looks. You're eating some grapes around the table with your nuclear family. Very casually, you hold a grape out for them to see and say something like, "Hey, check this grape out." Then, SWAP! You slam it down on top of your head. A shocked moment later, it pops out of your mouth.

You gotta love it.

Step 1. Pop a grape into your mouth when no one's paying any attention.

Step 2. Get another grape, with a little piece of stem still attached, and put it into your hand. Pinch the stem between your fingers so it doesn't show.

Step 3. After drawing everyone's attention to the grape in your hand, fake-toss it to your other hand. Since it is secretly stuck to your hand, you should be able to make this fake-toss look pretty convincing. (If you're a perfectionist, practice a few times by *really* tossing a grape hand to hand.)

Step 4. Slap your empty hand (the one everyone else thinks has a grape in it) down on top of your head.

Step 5. Look stricken for a moment. Then, suddenly, pop the other grape out of your mouth. Timing is everything.

Step 6. Smile.

Hand Jive

When two humans move into each other's personal space, a need exists for some kind of ice-breaking ritual. Grown-ups, of course, do the basic dead fish handshake: Grown-up A approaches Grown-up B. Grown-up A extends limp, sweaty hand. Grown-up B does the same, and the two rub their hands together clammily.

This is disgusting.

What follow are some alternatives that are vastly more interesting.

Slip Me Some Palm, Tom

Open hand behind back, bend knees slightly, rotate hips, present hand to "greetee" and groan appreciatively when he slaps it.

"Right ... Left ... High ... Low ... Too slow"

Hold hand open vertically to the right; greetee slaps it. Hold other hand open to the left, vertically; greetee slaps it. Hold hand open above head; greetee slaps it. Hold other hand open down low; greetee goes to slap it, but when he does, he misses because you jerked it out of the way. Accompany this little routine with the play-by-play commentary described in the title.

Right...

Left...

High...

Low...

Too slow!

The Styler, a Shake in Three Acts

Start with the normal "dead fish," but quickly switch to the "faith shake"...then the "hook shake"... and finally, part hands with a mutual fingersnap. The last bit, the mutual fingersnap, actually takes a bit of practice, but it's worth every minute.

1. Dead fish.

2. Faith shake.

3. Hook shake.

4. Mutual fingersnap.

"Grab My Thumb... Gee You're Dumb"

This is only for people who haven't achieved
my own high level of maturity in their humor
yet. Start by slapping fives. Do it palm to palm
("Give me five") and back of hand to back of
hand ("Other side"). Then hold an elbow up
high and get your victim to do the same. Bonk
elbows ("Give me a 'bow"). Switch elbows and
do it again ("One mo' "). Stick out your thumb,
get them to grab it ("Grab my thumb..."), and
when they do (fools that they are), hammer
them with the punchline (see title).

The Ankle Shake My personal favorite. Both parties approach each other and extend their hands fully, as if preparing for an ordinary but enthusiastic handshake. However, when the moment to grab hands arrives, both parties miss to the outside, and lean forward and down to take the other party's foot, which has been conveniently lifted for this very purpose. Foot is then shaken in the conventional manner. See illustration above.

Dairyman's Shake
Grab greetee by both thumb and forefinger and pull on each, alternately.

The Heart Association Shake Grab greetee with a firm hand, squeeze, and then relax ... and then squeeze ... and then relax ... and then squeeze ....

Upside-Down Water

This particular shenanigan runs extremely close to the Parent Approval Line. It may, in fact, cross over it in some isolated cases. Consider yourself warned. As usual with activities this close to the line, though, it is especially fine.

1. All you'll need is a glass of water, a cafeteria or dinner table, and a sheet of stiff paper. The table has to be smooth, with no tablecloth.

2. The glass should be reasonably full. Cover it tightly with the paper. Turn the glass over quickly—don't spill —and place it on the table upside down.

3. Hold the glass tight against the table and carefully withdraw the paper. Voila! An upside-down glass, full of water, sitting on your table!

4. Despite what your mother might say, this is not a mess waiting to be made, but instead an interesting physical conundrum. How does one remove the glass from the table without spilling all the water?

5. One possible solution (and there must be others) is to hold the glass tightly against the table and slide it carefully to the edge where you have a pitcher waiting. It will probably leave a snail's trail of wetness on the table, but this is a small price to pay for such an interesting problem.

Homemade Whoopee Cushion

I need hardly tell you how important the following information is. A well-made whoopee cushion tucked carefully underneath the sofa cushion is your ticket to lasting parental approval.

The balloon attached to this book is your key ingredient; plus the popsicle stick inside it.

Wedge the popsicle stick into the neck of the balloon as shown. This takes a little fooling around, but latex is incredibly forgiving. You'll get it eventually.

Blow the balloon up a little bit. The popsicle stick will make this a little hard, but fuss with it and you should be able to get four or five breaths in.

The neck should be stretched tight enough by the stick to keep the air from escaping.

Now. All you need to do is booby-trap a sofa or stuffed chair. Then, just before Dad gets home, put the evening paper right beside it.

Whoopee.

Fake a Sneeze

Yet another small but charming bit of business. This one comes to you directly from the campus of Franklin Elementary School, Summit, New Jersey, where it has enjoyed much popularity down through the years. Adults like it, but will not say so.

1. Dip your hand into the water from the drinking fountain.

2. Sneak up behind someone and fake the sound of an enormous, disgusting sneeze while simultaneously shaking the water from your wet hand onto the back of their neck.

3. Say "Bless me!"

How to Flip a Coin with Triumphant Style

The next time you're called upon to settle a dispute with a coin toss, here's an extremely impressive way to do it. Reach both hands into your pockets. Pull one out in a clenched fist. Open it to reveal an invisible nickel ("It's the only one I could find"). Let everyone get a good look at it.

Next, flip it high into the air. Very high. Then, "catch" it in the same hand as the one that did the tossing, and slap it onto the back of your other hand, in the traditional manner. Have someone call heads or tails.

When you pull off your hand to see who's won, everyone will miraculously find themselves looking at a real, non-invisible, nickel. For your part, don't miss a beat; announce either heads or tails (depending) and pocket the nickel with a smile.

Now, for the hardest part. DO NOT GIVE AWAY THE SECRET! This book will self-destruct if you do. Simply go on to whatever it was that led you to need a coin toss in the first place. Don't act surprised by your talents. In fact, act surprised that everyone else is surprised. That'll drive them wild.

For those of you who have to know the secret right away, here it is: *Style*. Magic is theater. Do it in a big way, or don't do it at all. Make all your movements oversized. When you lie about the invisible nickel, do it with a big smile and clear gaze. When you flip the coin, heave it way up there. When it "hits" your hand, you'll need sound effects, so snap your fingers (in the catching hand) at just the right instant. Then, when you finally reveal the nickel, make the unveiling as dramatic as you possibly can. Remember, this is show time. That's the real secret. What follows is just the technique, or handling.

The Moves

When you put both hands into your pockets, only one comes up empty. That's your "show" hand. The other one is the "guilty" hand; it has the nickel finger-palmed as shown.

Finger-palming is one of those life skills you really ought to learn. It enables you to keep a coin in a hand that looks innocently empty. (You never know when this might come in handy.)

Your task now is to get the nickel out of its finger-palmed hiding place and onto the back of that same hand. Invisibly. How? A secret little zip-toss. As you bring your two hands together for the final slap, seize that instant. As your guilty hand comes up to be slapped, get the nickel out of it by turning your hand and letting the nickel come loose. The coin should shoot out—faster than a speeding bullet—only to be intercepted— slapped back down—by your other hand, which is coming down open-palmed. The whole thing should be as quick as a wink.

Sounds tricky, doesn't it?

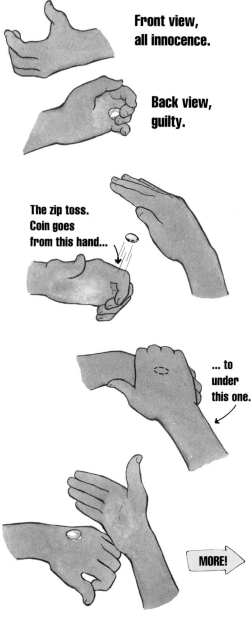

Front view, all innocence.

Back view, guilty.

The zip toss. Coin goes from this hand...

... to under this one.

MORE!

23

Relax. Here's a way to work into it slowly—a critical first step: Do the whole routine without any trickery. Get a real coin out of your pocket, really toss it high in the air, really catch it in the same hand as the one that tossed it, and really slap it back down onto the back of your other hand.

Do that five times and memorize every move. This will be boring but it's necessary.

Now, switch back to fakery. Try the whole routine with the invisible coin and the little zip-toss. Repeat. Repeat. And repeat again. Then, for a change of pace, do the whole bit again with a real coin and no trickery. Back and forth you should go. Fake it, then don't fake it. When the two versions look identical, you're there.

Tennis Ball Launcher

You'll need a basketball and a tennis ball. Stack them as 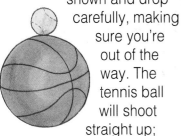 shown and drop carefully, making sure you're out of the way. The tennis ball will shoot straight up; the basketball will stop dead.

You can do the same thing, with even more impressive results, with a ping pong ball and a super ball (a super ball is one of those super bouncy rubber balls). If the super ball is as large as a tennis ball, place the ping pong ball on top of it and let the two of them go. Don't forget to stand back.

Flinch and Stink Eye

We stumbled across these games in an old volume entitled *Ghenghis Khan's Big Book of Fun*.

Just kidding.

Flinch is a playground basic with roots that go back to the barbarians. It's basically a test of reflexes with a little mild pain added for spice. You'll need two people. We'll start by making you the slapper, rather than the slappee.

1. Hold both hands, palms up, in front of you.

2. Have your partner, the slappee, lay his or her hands on top of yours, palm to palm.

3. Now begins the psychology. Your goal (as the slapper on bottom) is to slap the backs of your slappee's hands. This takes quick action. Their goal is to get out of the way. The tricky part is that you can fake as much as you like and if they go for a fake, you get a free slap.

4. If you really go for a slap, and they get away clean, switch places. A successful slap means everyone stays as they were.

Stink Eye (otherwise known as Stare Down) is a slightly more evolved version of Flinch. Put your nose exactly three inches from someone else's nose. Stare directly into his or her eyes and maintain an absolutely deadpan expression while your opponent does precisely the same. No talking and no moving of any facial muscles. First to crack is the loser.

Snapping Belt Loops

A small but satisfying piece of mischief. Perfect for those boring times when you're standing in another endless line staring at the back of some unsuspecting fool.

1. Shape your forefinger into a hook as shown. Keep it very stiff. Addressing the back of the person in front of you, say something like, "Do you mind if I tear your belt loop off? It's bothering me." Immediately snag their belt loop on the *tip* of your finger-hook. Pull firmly.

2. Before the person has a chance to mount a response, pull even harder and slip your finger-hook just a fraction *so that the tip of your finger slides off the loop.* The loop will pop hard into the crook of your finger. There will be a loud "snap" —exactly like the sound of a belt loop being torn off.

3. Your next line: "There. Doesn't that feel better?"

Dead Finger

Let's say you're outside fooling around when suddenly you find someone's dead finger, cut off and lying on the ground. Sound good? Of course it does. And then imagine the family's delight when you run inside and show it all around!

Well, here's a shenanigan that can make this dream come true.

You'll need an empty small box plus a bottle of baby powder or flour. Also a little red nail polish or ketchup, and a cotton ball or two.

Cut a hole in the bottom of the box. Pack it with cotton and smear the cotton with ketchup or nail polish. Then, powder up one of your forefingers until it looks dead white. For the final touch, smear some nail polish or ketchup tastefully over it. Stick it through the hole in the box and close the cover. Then run and find everyone and tell them a huge whopper about finding this box with the most disgusting thing you ever saw in your life inside. When everyone's gathered around, slowly open the box.

Paper Poppers

At the end of every lunch period in millions of schools everywhere, zillions of kids jump on top of their empty milk cartons in order to hear the loud bang they make when they explode. It's traditional.

What most of them don't know is that there exists a way to create this wonderful sound over and over again. It's called a paper popper, and here is how you make one.

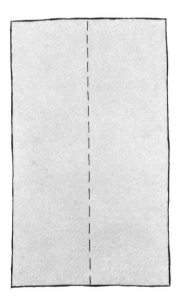

1. Make a crease down the center of your paper.

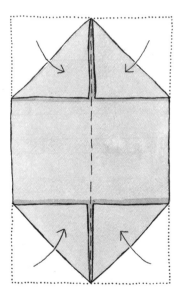

2. Fold in four corners as shown. Don't quite touch center crease.

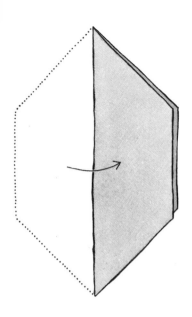

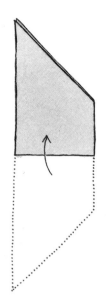

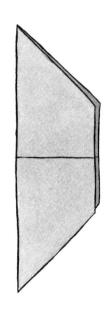

3. Fold in half as shown.

4. Fold as shown to make a horizontal center crease.

5. Unfold to show crease.

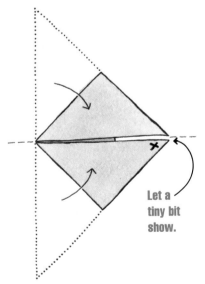

Let a tiny bit show.

6. Fold as shown.

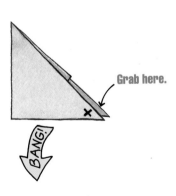

Grab here.

BANG!

7. Grab your popper tightly between thumb and forefinger at the "X." Act as if you were throwing a ball HARD straight down at your feet. At the end of that motion, snap your wrist, and the air should make the popper snap open (BANG!). It's like cracking a whip.

Hand Whistling

Everyone knows that you can blow across the opening to a bottle and create a low hooting sound. What they don't know is that you can do the same thing—only much better—with nothing but your hands.

The instructions that follow are guidelines and everyone who does it fools with it a little differently. A word of caution: This is not an instant success activity. It may take an hour, it may take days. But it's definitely worth the effort and once you've gotten it, you'll never be able to remember what made it so hard.

Hand whistling is a traditional musical form in South America. Especially in Bolivia, there are skilled hand whistlers who perform with bands and are occasionally flown up to U.S. recording studios. Hand whistling, practiced by a

master, has a haunting flute-like sound that no other instrument can duplicate. Even rank amateurs can achieve at least an octave range by fluttering their hands. Personally, I have a stirring rendition of *Camptown Races* that I would be happy to perform if only somebody would ask me.

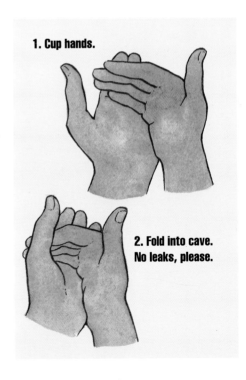

1. Cup hands.

2. Fold into cave.
No leaks, please.

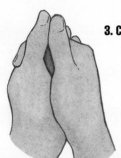

3. Create the opening.

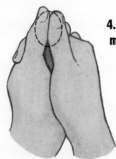

4. Poke out your lips, pucker up and place your mouth as shown by the dotted lines.

Two Minutes Later and You Can't Get It

You're probably doing two things wrong. One, you've got your hands smushed up to your mouth (Pucker up and poke those lips out!), and two, you're covering the entire opening of your "hand-cave." Bad habits, both of them.

Here's the key. You're playing the jug, not a trombone. You have to blow air *across* the hole. The whistle is created when the air-stream splits at the bottom of the opening—about half goes into your hand-cave, and half does not.

Lots of people find it helpful to dip their hands in water. It seals the leaks and makes their fingers taste better.

MORE

Two More Minutes and You <u>Still</u> Can't Get It

Poke out those lips! Imagine you're faced with a cakeful of candles and have to blow out only one of them. It's a precision air activity. If you're cheeks are puffed out, you're doing it wrong.

Everyone thinks the shape of their hand-cave is the critical thing. Actually, it's the shape and size of the opening and the angle at which your airstream hits it.

Last note: Try for a few minutes and then quit. Later on, when you're sitting in the back of the class, for example, try again. You'll stumble onto it and once you do, it's like riding a bicycle; you'll have it forever.

The Parent and the Egg

Simple, simple, simple. This is a great way to occupy a parent or older sibling for quite a little while. All you need are: (A) one parent or older sibling and (B) an egg.

Tell your helper that you have a magic trick you'd like to perform, but that in order to do it, you're going to need a brilliantly capable volunteer. Put your arm around the lucky person as you say this.

Now, open the front door halfway and stand the victim behind it. (You can also use the back door, but inside doors don't work; the bottom hinge is too low.) Get the person to reach their thumb and forefinger through the door crack just *above* the middle hinge. Then hand them an egg.

And leave.

You can come back from time to time to see how they're doing.

How to Sneak Around

Indoor Sneaking Around

The prime rule in sneaking around is this: Act at all times as if someone is *actively* looking for you. Even if you're sure no one knows what you're up to, pretend they do. This is known officially as "paranoia" and professional sneak-arounders swear by it.

When you're walking, step lightly, putting the ball of your foot down first. In hallways, you'll make fewer squeaks if you walk right next to the walls. This is especially true on stairs. Put your feet down right where the wall hits the stair, and support a lot of your weight on the rail, or, if you can reach it, the opposite wall.

On floors that don't squeak, move quickly when you're in the open and stop in doorways or behind open doors. When you're resting, it's important to stay absolutely silent in order to listen. Wait for a good minute (count to 60 slowly and silently) before moving on.

Take advantage of any noise you can. If you have to sneak by an open doorway and someone is inside the room, wait until they shuffle some papers or move around. The noise they make will cover you as you slide by the doorway. In the same vein, if the building is silent, listen for cars driving by, and move when they create some covering noise.

If you're in a room, stay close to the walls that are not directly opposite the door, so that a quick glance inside won't be enough to catch you. And be ready to freeze at the first sound. If you can duck noiselessly behind the couch, so much the better, but if you can't, you'll be amazed at what you can get away with by squatting down and staying absolutely silent and stock still in the shadows.

When you're sneaking around your own house, you have all the advantages. You should already know

which stairs or floorboards creak, so you can skip them. You should know which doors never get closed so that you can be ready to duck behind them instantly.

You should also know the best hiding place in every room. Getting under the bed might sound unimaginative, but grown-ups hate getting down on their knees, so it's a surprisingly good place. Or if the bedspread is all rumpled up anyway, just bury yourself underneath it and don't make a move or a sound.

In the bathroom, for a quick hiding spot, try stepping into the tub, squeezing up tight against the end wall (where the faucets are) and pulling the shower curtain out just enough to cover you.

Whenever you can get higher or lower than eye level, you're much harder to see. In some closets, you can take off your shoes and shinny

up toward the ceiling by putting your back against one wall and your feet against the other. You'll be amazed at how many people never look up when they walk into a closet.

In closets where you can't get high, get low. Squat down and stay absolutely silent, half-hidden in the coats or clothes. And another hint: Don't close the door. Leave it a little open. That way, you'll be able to hear if anyone's coming, you'll be able to leave without any noise, and a partway open door looks less suspicious anyway. (Incidentally, if you have to open or close a door, and you don't want it to squeak, take some weight off the hinges by lifting on the doorknob at the same time that you pull or push on it.)

If you're sneaking around some building with lots of people in it, just act as if you own the place. Stride purposefully ahead, just like everyone else does.

Outdoor Sneaking Around

It's time to restate the basic rule to sneaking around, since it's just as true outdoors as in: Always act as if someone is actively looking for you, even when you know that your target is completely oblivious. This kind of paranoia creates the right cautious attitude.

If you're shadowing someone in a quiet outdoor place, two things will attract their attention: noise and movement. Use covering noises as much as you possibly can. Wait for the wind to rustle the leaves before you move, and don't move when your suspect has stopped, or the noise you make will give you away.

Always be aware of your background. The worst possible background you can have is the sky. The best possible background is dark and shadowy, like trees and shrubbery. Also, stay as low as you have to. Don't stick up over your background. That means moving in a crouch, crawl, or even slither, depending on how close you are, and what's behind and in front of you.

Take advantage of every hiding spot you can, even small, shadowed spots if that's all there is. And avoid wide open spaces, even if you have to make large, semicircular detours to get around them.

If you're hiding behind a bush, tree, rock, car, or whatever, peek around the side of it, near the ground, not over the top. And look with just a single eye if you can—that way, the shape of your head won't be as obvious.

If you can remember only one tip for sneaking around outdoors, make it this one: Always be ready to freeze. Watch a cat sometime as it stalks a squirrel or a bird. Most of the time the cat is crouched and frozen, and never lets his eyes off his target. You should do exactly the same thing.

If you're following someone in a crowded, busy outdoor spot—like a street, park, or playground—you'll need to use different tactics. Now the best background for you is other people. As much as you can, walk with a crowd. In fact, if you can, team up with someone. Together, you'll attract less attention. And if you *do* separate, you'll be able to keep an eye on the target from different spots, which will enable one of you to break off and race ahead if necessary.

If you're trailing someone like your older sister who probably already knows what you look like, do it not just behind her, but behind her and across the street as well. An extra measure of safety goes a long way.

The Egg and Shirt Throw

A simple little exercise in the physics of high-speed eggs.

1. Find a long-sleeved shirt. Close off the neck opening by cinching it closed with a piece of string. Then knot off the sleeves. Leave it unbuttoned.

2. Get the owner of the shirt to hold it upside down by the tails. Get him to spread the shirt out a bit so that it's as wide as possible. (You want to make it wide because it is now no longer a shirt, but an egg target.) He should hold it to one side, like a matador's cape.

3. Get an egg. Back off a couple of feet. Rear back and throw the egg as hard as you possibly can into the shirt. Don't miss.

4. What happens? You'll have to try it yourself.

Phone Code

Every kid needs a code for messages that are too sensitive for grown-up eyes. What follows is a good basic code that should do the job nicely. It's based on the buttons on your phone, which look like this:

	ABC	DEF
1	2	3
GHI 4	JKL 5	MNO 6
PRS 7	TUV 8	WXY 9
*	OPER 0	#

Let's say you want to send this message in phone code:

Grounded for weekend unjustly. Bring ladder to window tonight at nine.

Here's how it would go:

The letter **G** is on the **4** button on your phone, and it's the number furthest to the left (GHI). So write **'4**. The letter **R** is on the **7** button, and it's in the middle (PRS), so write **7**. The letter **O** is on the **6** button (MNO), and it's the number furthest to the right, so write **6'**. When you get to the end of the word, put a slash. At the end of a sentence, two slashes. This is how the whole message would end up looking:

When it comes time to deliver your message, you might consider using an updated version of the bow-and-arrow system, which Robin Hood used to favor. Get an old tennis ball and cut a slit in it. Stick your message inside and toss it to your partner when the time is ripe. This is not as exciting as embedding a quivering arrow in a tree a few inches from your friend's head, but it carries less risk.

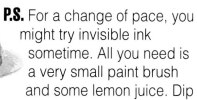

P.S. For a change of pace, you might try invisible ink sometime. All you need is a very small paint brush and some lemon juice. Dip the brush in the juice and write carefully on normal writing paper. After it dries, it will be invisible. You can read it by heating it carefully over a light bulb.

Pig Latin

Probably even more useful than something written, like the phone code, are spoken codes like Oppish and Pig Latin. Both of these are millions of years old and have been extensively field-tested on younger siblings and nosey grown-ups for millenia.

The easier of the two is Pig Latin. A very motivated eavesdropper *might* be able to figure it out, if it were not spoken very quickly, but for everyday espionage and sneakiness, Pig Latin is fine. Here is how it goes:

Rule: Take off the first consonant sound of a word, add "*ay*" to it and stick it on the end of whatever's left of the word.

For example: "Scram" becomes "*amscray.*" Why? Because I took the "*scr*" from the front of "scram," added "*ay*" to it and got "*scray.*" That left "*am*" from the original word, so I put "*scray*" on the end of it. Result? "*Amscray.*"

Confusing, isn't it? Here are a few more examples to make it worse.

television: *elevisiontay*
squirt: *irtsquay*
disgusting: *isgustingday*
klutz: *utzklay*

P.S. Words that start with vowels (aardvark, idiot, eggplant...) just get an "*ay*" stuck onto them (*aardvaarkay, idiotay, eggplantay*).

Oppish

Oppish might be even more popular than Pig Latin, although it's not as easy to master. However, once you do get up to speed on it, not even the CIA will be able to make any sense of you.

Rule: Insert "*op*" after the first consonant of any syllable. For example: "Road" becomes "*rop-oad*", "going" becomes "*gop-o-op-ing*" and "homeroom" becomes "*hop-ome- rop-oom.*"

Here's another example drawn from real life:

Before: Quick! Hide! Here comes my little brother.

After: *Quop-ick! Hop-ide! Hop-ere cop-omes mop-eye lop-it-top-le brop-o-thop-er!*

P.S. For words that start with vowels (aardvark, idiot, eggplant), put the first "*op*" right in front (*op-aard-vop-ark, opid-opi-opot, opegg-plopant*).

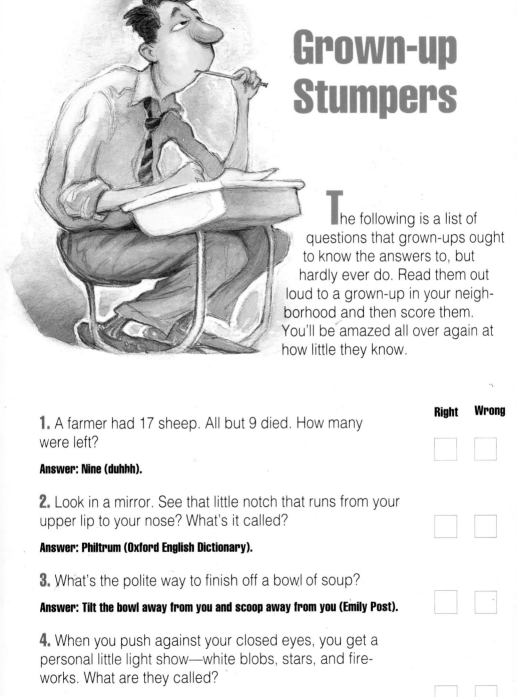

Grown-up Stumpers

The following is a list of questions that grown-ups ought to know the answers to, but hardly ever do. Read them out loud to a grown-up in your neighborhood and then score them. You'll be amazed all over again at how little they know.

	Right	Wrong

1. A farmer had 17 sheep. All but 9 died. How many were left?

Answer: Nine (duhhh).

2. Look in a mirror. See that little notch that runs from your upper lip to your nose? What's it called?

Answer: Philtrum (Oxford English Dictionary).

3. What's the polite way to finish off a bowl of soup?

Answer: Tilt the bowl away from you and scoop away from you (Emily Post).

4. When you push against your closed eyes, you get a personal little light show—white blobs, stars, and fireworks. What are they called?

Answer: Phosphenes (Webster's Ninth Dictionary).

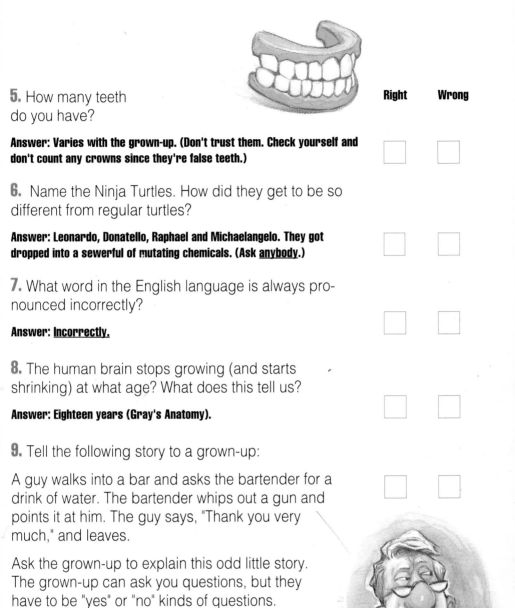

5. How many teeth do you have?

Right   Wrong

Answer: Varies with the grown-up. (Don't trust them. Check yourself and don't count any crowns since they're false teeth.)

6. Name the Ninja Turtles. How did they get to be so different from regular turtles?

Answer: Leonardo, Donatello, Raphael and Michaelangelo. They got dropped into a sewerful of mutating chemicals. (Ask <u>anybody</u>.)

7. What word in the English language is always pronounced incorrectly?

Answer: <u>Incorrectly.</u>

8. The human brain stops growing (and starts shrinking) at what age? What does this tell us?

Answer: Eighteen years (Gray's Anatomy).

9. Tell the following story to a grown-up:

A guy walks into a bar and asks the bartender for a drink of water. The bartender whips out a gun and points it at him. The guy says, "Thank you very much," and leaves.

Ask the grown-up to explain this odd little story. The grown-up can ask you questions, but they have to be "yes" or "no" kinds of questions.

Example: A <u>fair</u> question would be "Did the guy want to rob the bar?" An <u>unfair</u> question would be "What did the guy come into the bar for?"

Answer: The guy had the hiccups. He wanted to get rid of them with a glass of water. The bartender heard the hiccups, and as a favor, scared them out of the guy with a gun.

Don't Stop! There's more!

10. Hop in a plane in Tampa, Florida, and head due south. Where do you hit South America?

Right   **Wrong**

Answer: You don't. (See map).

☐   ☐

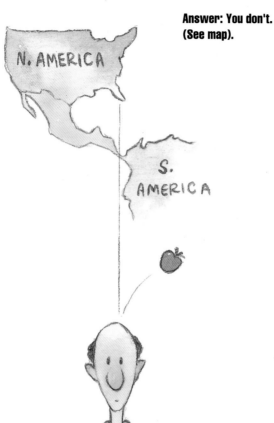

How to Grade Your Grownup

10 right.	Cheater. Probably peeked.
6-9 right.	Lucky guesser.
3-5 right.	Unlucky guesser.
0-2 right.	Typical.

48

Be Your Own Soda Can Bomb Squad

You're standing with a group of friends in the movie theater lobby. Someone hands you a can of soda pop. Suddenly, you appear to lose it. You start shaking the can violently up and down. Then, you thump it three or four good times with your forefinger and say "Sounds ripe to me," and immediately pull the pop top. Naturally, everyone scatters, screaming.

But what happens? Nothing. You take a drink from the can and look surprised. Where'd everyone go?

The secret is in the thumping. Better do a good job of it since all the bubbles that are so anxious to come squirting out all over your clothes are hanging on to the sides of the can like bats clinging to the ceiling of a cave. If you can knock them off the sides with a couple of good finger thumps, then they have to go back into the big bubble that's always at the top (where they came from before all the shaking). Once they're back up there, your can has been defused and you can open it fearlessly.

Fun in the Mail

to:
William Tell
35 Bowshot Dr.
Appleseed, Mn.
52311

You can mail strange things all by themselves —no envelope, no packaging of any kind —if you keep the following pointers in mind:

1. It can't be very big or very heavy (no bricks).

2. It can't break or fall apart, *no matter how much it gets thrown around* (no wine glasses).

3. It can't have any sharp points or edges to poke your mailman (no metal pointy things).

4. And finally, it helps a lot if the thing you're mailing is cute, goofy, or both. (We've had good luck with rubber bugs. It turns out that the post office *does* have a sense of humor. It's just repressed.)

Here are some suggestions: A teddy bear, a small piece of plywood or cardboard cut into a funny shape, a big rubber ball, a small stone, keys on a keychain, a plastic cup or dish, a rubber snake, a hair brush, a solid plastic toy, a sponge, an empty plastic jar, a shoe (no laces), etc. etc.

Use glue or staples to put the stamps on. If you cover them with tape, the post office will not deliver, because they can't cancel the stamps under tape. Use twice the amount of postage that the weight would indicate, and stick on the address label (and message, if you have any) with glue. Make the address label big and clear.

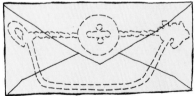

P.S. As long as we're on the subject of funny things in the mail, here's another sure-to-please idea. Find the following ingredients:

A pair of pliers
A good rubber band
A wire coat hanger
A big button
An envelope

1. Cut the rubber band and thread it through the big button. Then, with your pliers, bend off a length of coat hanger and shape it carefully into a "C." Tie the rubber band on as shown and wind it up fairly tightly.

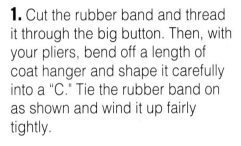

2. Then stick the whole arrangement, still wound up, into the envelope, rubber band side up. Look at the picture and pay attention to it.

3. Seal the envelope (the band should not unwind) and mark very clearly: "Rattlesnake Eggs. KEEP REFRIGERATED!" You can hand-deliver this little surprise package, or mail it. Your choice. In either case, be confident your package will truly have an impact.

Kid Facts

A Selection of Important Information for Kids

1. If you chew Wintergreen LifeSavers in the dark with your mouth open, they make visible sparks.

2. If you break or lose an inexpensive toy, or drop a candy bar or ice cream cone in the dirt, or experience any similar sort of disaster, many companies will send you a coupon or a freebie if you write them nicely and tell them what happened and how sad you are because you really like their stuff. Write the letter yourself and address it "President" (you don't have to know the person's last name). Find the street address on the package. And draw a picture of yourself on the envelope.

to: The President
CRunchy, INc,
33 Dewsop Lane
39112
(me)

3. If you write to the Chocolate Manufacturers Association of America (7900 Westpark Drive, Suite A-230, McLean, VA 22102), they will send your parents a free pamphlet explaining that chocolate is a lot better for you than you think (it does *not* cause pimples, for example).

4. Sneezes travel at better than 100 miles per hour.

5. Trying to read in the dark does not ruin your eyes.

6. A lady once fell out of an airplane at 30,000 feet and lived.

7. A lady in Alabama once got hit by a meteorite. It came through her roof and bounced off her radio. It didn't kill her.

8. A guy in France once ate seven TV sets and in four days ate a supermarket cart. He once ate a bike and said that his favorite part was the chain ("the only part with any taste").

9. One of the richest ladies in Texas, the daughter of a former governor, was named Ima Hogg. She did not have a sister named Ura.

10. You can figure how far away a lightning bolt struck by counting seconds after the flash until the thunder (one one thousand, two one thousand, three one thousand...). Figure 1,000 feet per second, or 5 seconds per mile.

11. You can't get your eyes stuck in the crossed position.

12. If you and another person say the exact same thing, at the exact same time, and it's not on purpose, hook pinkies and silently make wishes. They will come true.

Body Weirdnesses and Tongue Gymnastics

Almost everybody has something they can do with their body that makes everyone else sick. For many people, how weird their bodies are is a matter of enormous pride. Fortunately, modern science has looked into this area—the double-jointed, crossed-eyes, curled-tongue branch of medical science—and discovered the following:

▲ True ear wigglers are in the minority. Only 20% of the male population and 10% of the female population can do it. Be forewarned, however, that many people will just work their jaw around and claim they are wiggling their ears. This is false, and these people should be discouraged. Also know that true ear wigglers can almost invariably roll their tongue as well.

▲ If you can curl your tongue into a tube, don't get too excited; 85% of the population can. It's hereditary.

▲ If you can stand your tongue up on one edge, vertically, and then flop it over so it's standing up on the other edge, that's a little more impressive. Now we're talking maybe one person out of three.

▲ If you can form the tip of your tongue into the shape of a "W," you are in rare company. The numbers are too small to even measure statistically. Consider yourself a Tongue Legend.

▲ Harpo Marx, in the movie "Animal Crackers," formed a bubble on the end of his tongue and then blew it off, intact, into the air. In human history, this is the only documented performance of the "Free Floating Tongue Bubble," once thought to be only a myth.

▲ Have you ever wanted to push your finger all the way through your head? But you've been stumped because you didn't know how? Well, here are the easy-to-follow directions.

Push your forefinger into your ear and grunt and groan as you struggle to poke it all the way through. Then, with a sudden effort, bend it at the first joint (away from the audience) so it looks like you've broken through the ear drum and achieved a startling success. To complete the tasteful effect (and this is the real key) stick your tongue into your cheek simultaneously with the break-through. Now it ought to look as if your finger is poking your cheek out (get it?). Move your hand around a bit and simultaneously move your tongue to strengthen the appearance. If you practice this in front of a mirror so that it looks perfect, know that you are a very immature person.

▲ For most people, the most ticklish part of their body is the roof of their mouth.

▲"Striking red hair" is found on less than 2% of the population. Hair on the crown of the head grows clockwise 90% of the time. Lefties are a 7% minority.

▲ Regarding the belly button. Approximately 10% of kids are "outies." Grown-ups are almost all "innies."

Dollar Ring

This is a compelling project. Do not skip it, even if you normally don't like little crafty things—*This one is different.* You'll be working with real money (always exciting), and when you're finished you can parade around with an extremely eye-catching little ring—permanent, too—at least until that weak moment when you give in and spend it.

P.S. Don't worry about the instructions. They may seem long, but that's because we tend to be painfully clear. Nothing is assumed. Everything is illustrated. Just take it step by step. It's really not that bad.

1. Go get a nice, crisp one-dollar bill. An old limp bill is worthless. Don't even try.

2. Lay your bill on a tabletop with George rightside up and facing you. Fold the back bottom margin toward you and crease it down firmly. (Note I said *back* bottom margin. The back margins are a little bigger than the front.) For this fold—and all the folds that follow—use a pencil or something to crease them well. And be *precise*. Neatness counts.

Fold up the back bottom margin. Firmly crease it down flat.

3. Fold the top half down to cover the bottom, but don't bring it down quite all the way. Leave it short of the bottom edge by just a hair. As always, finalize the crease well with a pencil.

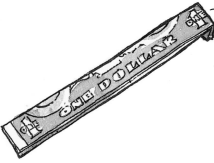

4. Now fold the top half down again. This time, though, bring it perfectly to the edge.

5. Turn the bill over and fold the right margin under.

6. Now fold the left side up exactly as illustrated. The "N" in ONE should be exactly half-visible when you're done.

7. Next, flip the vertical part over, as shown. Crease well.

MORE!

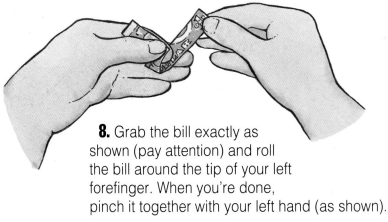

8. Grab the bill exactly as shown (pay attention) and roll the bill around the tip of your left forefinger. When you're done, pinch it together with your left hand (as shown).

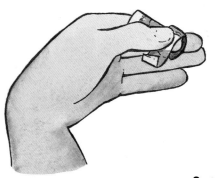

KEY POINT:
The dimensions "A" and "B" have to be the same.

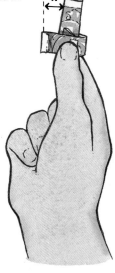

9. Switch hands and hold the bill as shown.

10. Now, fold down the vertical part of the bill. (Lift up your thumb in order to do this and put it back down when you're done.)

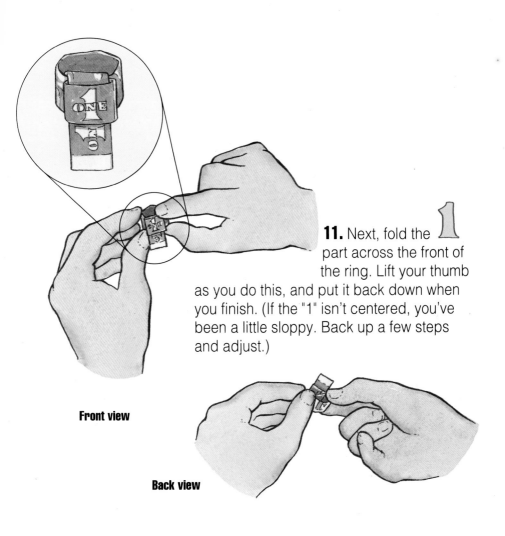

11. Next, fold the ![1] part across the front of the ring. Lift your thumb as you do this, and put it back down when you finish. (If the "1" isn't centered, you've been a little sloppy. Back up a few steps and adjust.)

Front view

Back view

12. Let go of the ring (don't worry, I know what I'm doing) and it should partially unfold to look like this. Now you can do a taper fold if you want. It's optional, but it makes a more finished-looking ring. If you don't want it, skip ahead to step 14.

The taper fold

13. Roll up the edge of the bill directly under the two "L"s of "DOLLAR". Crease it down, then do it again on the top edge, directly above it. Use a pencil to make the creases permanent. Once that's done, you're ready to go back to where you were.

14. Reassemble the ring to exactly what you had before I told you to let it unfold (step 11). It should look like this:

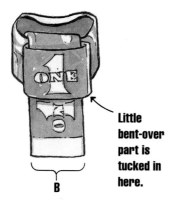

Little bent-over part is tucked in here.

B

15. Now you have to keep the  from popping up. To do that, tuck in the little bent-over part under "B." Now you're getting close. Smooth everything and crease well.

16. The next to last step. Turn the ring over. The backside of it has a diagonal slot. Tuck "B" into it as shown. Use a pencil point since this is close work. Keep it neat! The dotted lines show how the ring back is shaped when the taper fold (the optional step) is done.

B

Tuck "B" into slot.

17. Now all that's left is the finish work. Use your pencil to rub down the rolled edges. Very nice.

You're done. Wear it with pride. Note that it doesn't really fit grown-ups very well. Their fingers are too fat.

The Coat Hanger and the Coin

This is one of the hardest shenanigans in this book. It *can* be done, but it takes faith, patience, coordination, courage, and a quarter. Don't go into this one expecting instant gratification. It may take ten minutes, it may take a day, but it's worth whatever you have to put into it. The end result is incredible.

Warning: There is an excellent chance that you will send a coat hanger flying during this activity, so CLEAR OUT THE AREA FIRST!

Procedure:

1. Find a wire coat hanger whose tip was cut flat. Then bend the hanger into a diamond shape.

Flat tip important!

2. Borrow a quarter.

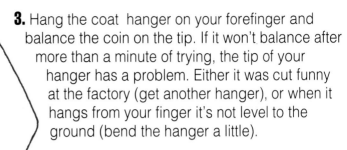

3. Hang the coat hanger on your forefinger and balance the coin on the tip. If it won't balance after more than a minute of trying, the tip of your hanger has a problem. Either it was cut funny at the factory (get another hanger), or when it hangs from your finger it's not level to the ground (bend the hanger a little).

4. Finally you've balanced the quarter. Amazing. But that's only the start. Gently start rocking the hanger back and forth on your finger. (Gently!) Rock it back and forth three or four times, each time a little more strongly, until (deep breath) you make the Big Swing, all the way around. Do this firmly, smoothly, fearlessly. (Only one spin direction works. Check the illustration.)

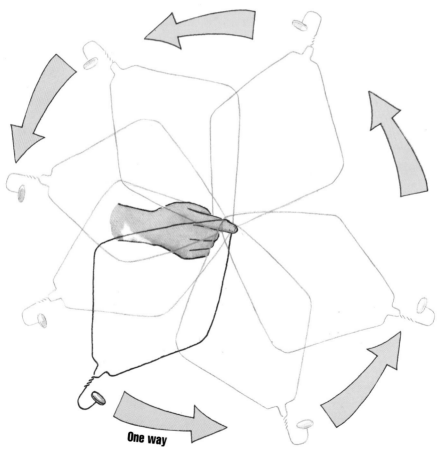

One way

Once you're up to speed, keep spinning. Don't panic! Now you have to stop it.

5. Yes it's true, you can stop the hanger with the coin still on. Unfortunately, this is almost impossible to describe in a readable way. You have to slow the hanger down from full speed to a dead stop in one-half of a revolution, by stretching your arm and taking a giant step *in the direction of the swing.*

6. Confused? Of course you are— I told you it wasn't readable. Try this slow-down technique with the coat hanger *but no coin.* That should help take the pressure off. Then put the coin back in place and try again. And again. And again. Write me when you get it.

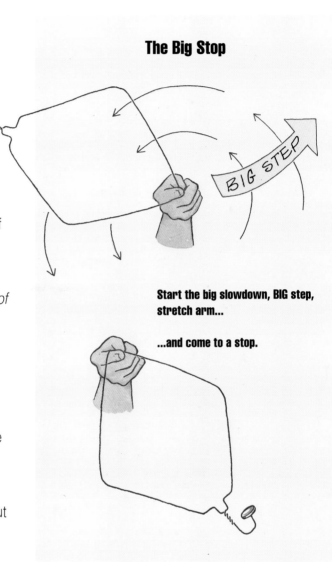

The Big Stop

Start the big slowdown, BIG step, stretch arm...

...and come to a stop.

The Automatic (Systematic) Articulated Mop and Spring-Loaded Broom-Driven Pie Tin Flier and Egg Dropper

EARLY MACHINE

Humans are toolmakers. It is this ceaseless need to invent, perhaps more than any other single quality, that distinguishes our species from all others. Beginning with the wheel, the spear, and the crude longbow, humans have been inventors for millions of years. It is our destiny.

While the story of Man the Machine Maker is an ancient one, it has also been one of unrelenting progress. From the first simple club, right up to today's jet engines and popcorn poppers, our increasingly sophisticated machines have reflected our improving understanding of the physical world around us.

Today, looking back over all of this, many leading scientists have wondered if this process is open-ended, or if there might not be some Final Understanding leading to an "ultimate machine" that could incorporate everything that people have learned—or in fact could ever learn—about the laws of the physical universe.

This is a very deep question, metaphysical in its implications, but here in front of you are the drawings that we believe will finally put it to rest. Because we believe that here on this fold-out is technology's Holy Grail, the culmination of 6,000 years of human thought and invention: *The Automatic (Systematic) Articulated Mop and Spring-Loaded Broom-Driven Pie Tin Flier and Egg Dropper.*

Consider for a moment how this marvelous machine is designed to operate:

1. Mother angrily enters through door, knocking over first book.

2. Book knocks over all the other books and tower.

3. Mop falls, pulling out pendulum prop.

4. Rubber-band-loaded pendulum snaps down and pops balloon with pin.

5. Pinched string is released.

6. Weight falls, pulling string trigger, releasing golf ball.

7. Golf ball rolls down cardboard trough.

8. Golf ball falls into cup knocking out prop.

9. Rubber-band-loaded broom snaps forward, sending pie tin flying.

10. Pie tin knocks out cardboard tube under egg.

11. Egg splashes down into glass of water. Unbroken.

The Paper Cup Trigger

Spring-load the broom with rubber bands or bungie cord as shown. Don't be afraid to really do a job here with a good number of big rubber bands (or bungie cord). You want that broom to snap down *hard*. Prop it away from the table with a strip of cardboard that has been inserted into a paper cup as shown. This is tricky—the broom should be under considerable tension. The cardboard trigger gets wedged in between the broom and the edge of the table. When you're done, the trigger should be in place, but just barely. One touch from the golf ball, and *WHAM!* Test once or twice before moving on.

pie tin

cardboard strip is stuck through cup

big rubber bands (or bungie cord)

The Water Glass, Tube and Egg Subassembly

It's precision time again. You have to arrange and locate this subassembly pretty carefully. When the broom slams against the table, it has to hit that pie tin square, so it can send it flying. But, on the other hand, the drinking glass has to be out of harm's way.

Don't stick egg into tube! Balance it!

pie tin

overhangs table edge

The trick is to position the glass just in from the edge, so that the pie tin overhangs but the glass is safe. Make sure that the cardboard tube that sits on the pie tin is centered *directly* over the glass. Squat down and look this over carefully. Then gently set the egg on top of the tube, not nestled down into it. If the egg gets stuck even a little into the tube and you pull the trigger—we disavow any knowledge of these instructions.

The Paper Plate Pulley

The biggest secret to this subassembly is that it's entirely unnecessary. We're including a drawing of it here because we went to the significant trouble of building it and wanted everybody to know it. Plus we like the high-tech look of it. But if you can't follow the drawings, or can't find the ingredients, or just don't care about appearances—skip it. Hang the onion over the edge of the chair and that'll work fine.

Tape the plates together.

to the golfball trough

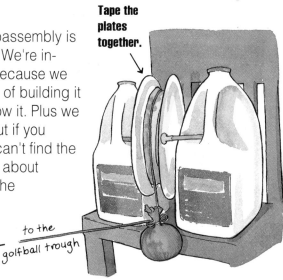

The Golfball Trough

Cut out the corners of a cardboard box as shown in the illustrations and tape them all together to make one long trough. Set it up on neat little cardboard trestles like we have in the illustration, or just fake it with a few books. Adjust the slope of the trough so that the golfball *slowly* rolls along. It's much more dramatic that way. Test a few times by itself to make sure the ball doesn't get hung up along the way.

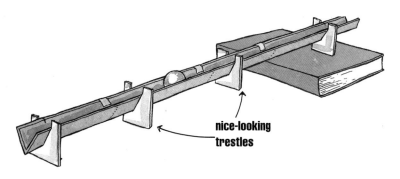

nice-looking trestles

Properly built and maintained, the ASAMSLBDPTFED Machine will work day or night, taking about 25 awe-inspiring seconds from first trigger to final egg plop. In our test laboratories, we can build one in 30 minutes or so, but you should figure on twice that.

Also, figure on a quite a little treasure hunt assembling all the ingredients.

You will find that repairs to the ASAMSLBDPTFED machine are quite straightforward, since all

the moving parts are completely exposed. In that same vein, expect to have to make a few repairs, especially at first during the de-bugging phase. We strongly recommend a couple of test runs before you bring in an audience.

List of ingredients:

One chair

One table

One broom

One mop

Two or three corrugated cardboard boxes

Ten heavy-duty rubber bands (or two bungie cords)

Fourteen big books (like encyclopedias)

One ball of string

One thumb tack

One balloon

Two phone directories

Two pencils or chopsticks

One roll masking tape

One onion

One golf ball

One paper cup

One half-filled, wide-mouthed drinking glass

One pie tin

One egg

Paper Plate Pulley Ingredients (optional):

Two paper plates

Two half-gallon containers full of milk or water

Chopstick or pencil

Even though this is a pretty mundane list, you will never be able to find 100% of it in one house. If it's any consolation, we never could either. Fortunately, this is an incredibly flexible design. Practically everything in this list can either be skipped, faked, fudged, or substituted for. We know, because we did it. What you see here is the idealized version, probably unreachable in the real world. What we did—and what you should do—is improvise. If you can't come up with something, figure out what it's for (not hard) and substitute. The only exception to this is the egg. You have to have one. Nothing else will do.

Assembly Instructions

For the most part, just look at the drawings and figure it out. If you get stuck, read the pointers below.

The Balloon Box Subassembly

The idea here is to stick a balloon into a box so tightly that you can trap a string between the balloon and the inside of the box. That way, when the balloon pops, the string will be released.

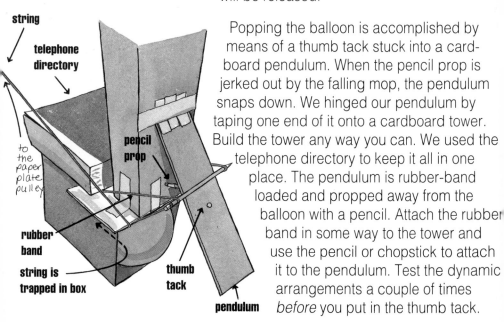

Popping the balloon is accomplished by means of a thumb tack stuck into a cardboard pendulum. When the pencil prop is jerked out by the falling mop, the pendulum snaps down. We hinged our pendulum by taping one end of it onto a cardboard tower. Build the tower any way you can. We used the telephone directory to keep it all in one place. The pendulum is rubber-band loaded and propped away from the balloon with a pencil. Attach the rubber band in some way to the tower and use the pencil or chopstick to attach it to the pendulum. Test the dynamic arrangements a couple of times *before* you put in the thumb tack.

string
telephone directory
to the paper plate pulley
pencil prop
rubber band
string is trapped in box
thumb tack
pendulum